Teaching English as a foreign language
A practical guide

Colin Dawson MA(Oxon.)

Nelson

Thomas Nelson and Sons Ltd
Nelson House   Mayfield Road
Walton-on-Thames   Surrey
KT12 5PL   UK

51 York Place
Edinburgh
EH1 3JD   UK

Thomas Nelson (Hong Kong) Ltd
Toppan Building 10/F
22A Westlands Road
Quarry Bay   Hong Kong

© Colin Dawson 1984
First published by George G. Harrap and Co. Ltd 1984
(under ISBN 0-245-53929-8)

Second impression published by Thomas Nelson and Sons Ltd 1985
ISBN 0-17-444200-9
NPN 19 18 17 16 15 14 13 12 11 10
Printed in Hong Kong

All Rights Reserved. This publication is protected in the
United Kingdom by the Copyright Act 1956 and in other
countries by comparable legislation. No part of it may
be reproduced or recorded by any means without the
permission of the publisher. This prohibition extends (with
certain very limited exceptions) to photocopying and similar
processes, and written permission to make a copy or copies
must therefore be obtained from the publisher in advance.
It is advisable to consult the publisher if there is any doubt
regarding the legality of any proposed copying.

Acknowledgements

I should like to thank my wife for unfailing encouragement and
support; my children for regularly challenging my use of English;
and Marjorie Sweetko, an inspiring teacher and teacher trainer
of English as a foreign language.

Contents

Introduction	5
Communication in the classroom	**9**
1 How to get your students talking	9
2 Seating arrangements	10
3 Chorus work and pair work	12
4 Asking and answering questions	13
5 Dialogues	14
What to teach – the basics	**17**
6 Planning a lesson	17
7 Vocabulary	19
8 Grammar	21
9 Pronunciation	23
Ways and means	**26**
10 Visual materials	26
11 Using pictures	27
12 Realia	29
13 Recorded material	31
14 Practice in listening	33
15 Language laboratories	35
16 Drills	37
17 Textbooks	38
18 Handouts and worksheets	40
19 Prose passages	41
20 Extensive reading	42
21 Authentic material	44
22 Dictation	46
23 Writing (up to intermediate level)	47
24 Post-intermediate writing – composition	48
25 Marking written work	50
26 Testing	51
27 Preparing for an external examination	52
28 Games and songs	53

| 29 | Discussions | 55 |
| 30 | Outings | 56 |

Appendix 59
Examination boards 59
Teacher training for English language teachers 61
Some recommended books 62
Useful addresses 64

Introduction

The aim of this book is to give you practical advice about how to teach English as a foreign (or second) language, using English as the language of instruction. It concentrates on method in the classroom.

1 Your language and the student

Using English in order to teach English makes heavy demands on your concentration, because you have to match your language to the level that the class understands. When you go from one level of class to another, you have to 'change gear'. This somewhat unnatural process is, at first, especially difficult for native English speakers.

Learning English also makes heavy demands on the students' concentration. They have to put aside their own language and work entirely in English. They have to listen carefully to new sounds, learn a whole range of new words, and accustom themselves to new sentence patterns. Like most students, they are reluctant to say that they do not understand the lesson, and you will have to be particularly careful to test whether they have really understood. It's no use asking them, 'Do you understand?', because they will probably just nod and smile at you, giving the impression that they do understand, whether this is true or not. So you must ask them to *use* or *explain* what you have been teaching them. This important point is taken up again in the section on grammar (chapter 8).

In the classroom you should try to:
- speak clearly and concisely (but not so slowly that natural rhythm and pronunciation are destroyed).
- adapt the level of your language to the class you are teaching.
- test stage by stage whether your students understand what you are teaching.

2 Your students

A variety of needs
Students come to your classes with different needs and different reasons for learning English. Some want to be able to speak, read

Introduction

and write. Others are only interested in speaking. Ideally we would separate students with different needs and different goals, but in practice this cannot often happen.

Whatever the students' needs, most theorists and practising teachers agree that the spoken word is the basis for teaching all other aspects of English. Speaking will therefore remain central in your teaching at all levels.

At beginner level, most of the work has to be oral (the written word being used mainly to confirm and clarify). It is at intermediate level that the students' different needs have to be taken into consideration. Group work within the class may be necessary and homework, if set, may vary from one group to another. There is no point setting the whole class imaginative essays if half the class is only interested in writing business letters.

Student levels
This book refers to four levels:

ABSOLUTE BEGINNERS: know a few words of English or none at all.

FALSE BEGINNERS OR LOW INTERMEDIATE: have learned some English before and are able to speak, read and write at a very basic level. Speech may be better than reading or writing.

INTERMEDIATE: able to progress, after six months or a year, to an examination like the Cambridge First Certificate.

ADVANCED: have passed an examination like the Cambridge First Certificate.

Mixed attainment classes
Sometimes you are faced with a class of both beginners and intermediate students, each group being too small to make up a class of its own.

There is no point in trying to ignore the differences in attainment. Some **group work** is inevitable, that is, you will have to teach one group, while other groups are working by themselves on tasks suited to their level.

There should be times, however, when the whole class works as one unit, otherwise it will cease to be a class. When you want to teach all students together, you have to choose activities – such as an oral composition based on pictures – where they can all make a contribution. Each student will tell the story at his or her own level. Later in the lesson or for homework, intermediate students can write their own version of the story, while the beginners will need more help.

You may also find that some **pair work** is possible between two students of different levels of attainment. For example, in some conversations one role is harder or longer than another. Or perhaps the lower level students could *read* their part of a conversation, while the higher level students would be expected to remember theirs.

A great deal depends on the cooperative spirit in the class. Your main duty as the teacher, however, is to see that *all* students make progress.

3 Your own teaching

Here are four ways in which you can become a better teacher:
- Invite an experienced teacher to observe some of your lessons. Discuss them frankly afterwards.
- Observe the lessons of an experienced teacher.
- Keep up to date with developments in language teaching by reading and by taking part in in-service training courses (see appendix 2).
- Arrange for a video-recording to be made of you and your class while you are teaching. Study the recording carefully.

More detailed advice, about techniques of teaching, is to be found in the various sections of this book, but there are two general points that I would like to emphasize. To be an effective teacher you need:
- a genuine interest in your students.
- a sense of humour.

Good luck in your teaching!

Colin Dawson

1 Communication in the classroom

How to get your students talking

1 If the main aim of your course is **oral fluency**, you have to organize lessons so that students *speak English as much as possible*.

2 In a traditional grammar-based lesson, students read aloud passages from textbooks and read out answers to written comprehension questions. This is *not* oral work. Each student, in this kind of lesson, would speak on average for only about two minutes per lesson.
Two minutes' speaking time per lesson is not enough.

3 Speaking time can be vastly increased by **chorus work** and **pair work** (chapter 3), but there are other possibilities from the moment the students enter the class:
- talk to the students as they come in. Don't let five minutes go by, waiting for the whole class to arrive.
- provide interesting things for them to talk about, for example, a colourful poster, a bunch of keys, (see chapters 10, 11 and 12).
- insist that they talk to each other in English and not in their native language(s).
- encourage them to help and correct each other, rather than always asking you, the teacher, to help.

4 Students will be more willing to speak if:
- they have something interesting to talk about.
- they feel that you are genuinely interested in them as people.
- the aim of speaking is real *communication*; in other words, the students will be more interested in replying to a question to which they think you do *not* know the answer. For example, '*Where is your friend today, Maria?*' is better than a mechanical question like '*What is on the desk?*'

5 Correcting your students' speech
There are no hard and fast rules but, generally:
- correct them when they make a mistake over some specific language point which they are currently learning, or are supposed to know.
- do *not* correct them if they are engaged in general conversation, *as long as what they are trying to communicate is clear*.

You should, however, make a note of their errors and bring in the necessary revision as soon as possible.

Teaching English as a foreign language

Seating arrangements

If *real communication* is to take place in the classroom, the students must be seated accordingly:

1 If you insist on the traditional layout of chairs and desks (layout A), the only communication you are going to get is a formal exchange of question and answer from the teacher to one student at a time.

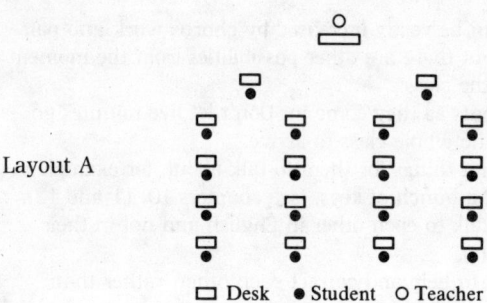

Layout A

☐ Desk ● Student ○ Teacher

2 With layout B communication is improved because:
- by coming out from behind her desk, the teacher clearly invites and expects the students to communicate.
- the students respond to the lack of formality by relaxing. At the same time they have the security of being behind a desk (and a convenient writing surface).
- students can see each other. They are not looking at the back of each other's heads. Eye-contact improves communication.
- pair work is easily arranged (chapter 3).

Communication in the classroom

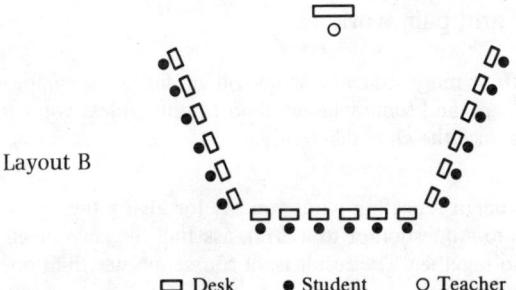

Layout B

☐ Desk   • Student   ○ Teacher

3 More informal layouts are possible: dispensing with desks altogether (layout C), seating the students in groups, or in one or two circles (for discussion) and so on. The main criterion is that the layout is *appropriate to the classroom activity*. Obviously one cannot keep changing the layout, but layout A will be necessary, for example, for a formal test.

4 In classes where there are both beginners and intermediate students, some **group work** is necessary and the seating areas must be appropriate.

5 Large classes (over 16 students) make oral work more difficult and the only effective way is to arrange group work, that is, one half of the class does written work while you do oral work with the other half. Rearranging the seating with a lot of furniture and students is not always easy, but it is worth the effort. The students will help you.

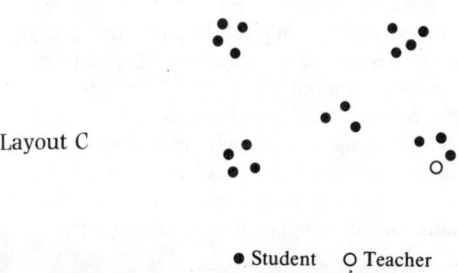

Layout C

• Student   ○ Teacher

Teaching English as a foreign language

Chorus work and pair work

1 In classes of 16 or more students, some will get far less speaking practice than others, and some will get almost none, unless you take steps to organize the class differently.

2 Chorus work
Instead of one student repeating what you say (or giving the correct response to a question or to a drill), ask half the class or all the class to do so together. The result is, of course, noisier than one student speaking, but:
- half or all of the class is involved, not just one student.
- the weak or shy students join in without embarrassment.

Chorus work is particularly good with beginners and low intermediate students. The teacher's job is to organize the class so that they know when and how to respond in chorus – practice and humour are needed! Sometimes you need to beat time to keep them all together. Some uninhibited conducting is required.

After the chorus work, do some individual checking, because errors made by the quieter students during chorus work are hard to detect.

3 Pair work
After you have presented a new item of grammar, vocabulary or pronunciation, the students need to practise it orally. Ask them to work in pairs so that they can go over material together, changing roles after a while. Meanwhile, you go round the class listening to each pair, checking that the work is being done.

EXAMPLE 1
You have just taught the second conditional. In pairs, the students ask each other a number of prepared questions which you have written on the board or on a handout:

'If you had six months' holiday, what would you do?'

'If you were able to choose, would you be a man or a woman?'

There would be four or five questions like these. Student A asks student B the questions and then perhaps adds one or two of his/her own, on the same model. Student B then becomes the questioner.

EXAMPLE 2 (to practise the present continuous tense)

Student A: *'Where is she going?'* (shows a picture)
Student B: *'Oh, she's going to the launderette.'*

4 Yes, it is quite noisy! But a great deal of speaking practice is going on which you would otherwise be quite unable to organize without a language laboratory. And they *can* all be asked to talk quietly!

Asking and answering questions

1 A great deal of communication takes place by asking and answering questions. In real life, we normally ask questions to which we do *not* know the answer. In language classes, as in most teaching, we (the teachers) have to ask questions to see if the student knows the answer and can express it grammatically.

As in all other aspects of teaching, variety is important. We should ask our students to:
- give information (to show understanding).
  Where was X going?
  (He was going) to the cinema.
- use vocabulary that is being learned.
  Which room do you have breakfast in?
  In the dining room.
- use a specific grammatical construction.
  What did he accuse X of doing?
  He accused him of eating the last cake.
- practise pronunciation (the short 'i' or /I/).
  Where do you live?
  I live in Ipswich.

You need to phrase your question carefully to get the answer you want.

2 In language teaching we should avoid questions which can be answered by *Yes* or *No*, because this means that the teacher says ten words to the student's one. We should try to reverse this position and ask **open-ended questions** like:
  Why . . . ?
  What did she do then? (And then . . . ?)
  What would have happened if . . . ?

3 Students must *ask* questions too. For the purposes of everyday communication, the ability to *ask* a question is more useful than the ability to answer.

4 The formation of questions in English needs careful explanation and regular practice up to intermediate level. A good method is to give these kinds of instruction to a student:

a Jose, ask Maria if she is going out tonight.
(Jose: *'Maria, are you going out tonight?'*)

b Ahmed, ask Mohammed if he knew that the new teacher had arrived.
(Ahmed: *'Mohammed, did you know that the new teacher had arrived?'*)

c Carole, ask Xavier what the time is.
(Carole: *'Xavier, what time is it?'*)

To reduce the number of words used by the teacher, keep instructions short:

a Jose – Maria – out tonight

b Ahmed – ask Mohammed – new teacher – arrive

c Carole – Xavier – time

Students soon get used to the idea of this 'spoken shorthand'. As well as learning how to form questions (word order, change of tense and so on), students also learn different intonation patterns (chapter 9).

Dialogues

1 The advantages

Dialogues are usually a much better source of oral work than prose passages. They are particularly good for pronunciation practice. If you have to use a textbook which has few dialogues, or none at all, it is worthwhile making up your own or finding dialogues from another source.

2 Characteristics of a good dialogue

For beginners and intermediate classes, these are:
- it is not too long (12–20 lines).
- it has two or three speakers only.
- it is fairly realistic (situation and language).

- it does not introduce too much new material.
- it contains one or two new grammar points, each illustrated two or three times.

Good commercially recorded dialogues have added sound effects for extra realism (chapter 13).

3 How to use dialogues

A tried and tested method, but not the only one:

a Let the class *hear* the dialogue before they see it written down. One of these methods can be used:
  - play a pre-recorded tape.
  - read out the dialogue yourself, changing your tone of voice for a different speaker. You could also change your position, or put on and take off a hat to show a change of character!
  - if you have an exceptionally good student, ask him/her to read one part with you.

b After the students have heard the dialogue once, ask a few *simple* questions about it.

c Play or read the dialogue again.

d Ask some more searching questions, perhaps bringing in the use of one of the grammar points.

e Let the students see the dialogue written down.

f Play or read the dialogue once again, while they follow it in print.

g Now highlight the pronunciation, vocabulary and grammar that form the basis of this part of the lesson.

h Pay special attention to the intonation and stress of key words and phrases.

4 Follow-up – some ideas

- dialogues can be acted out in pairs (chapter 3).
- memory can be tested by letting the students hear or see one role and asking them to supply the other, (particularly good for pair work or for work in the language laboratory).
- some shorter dialogues can be learnt by heart.
- the same framework can be used to ask the students to construct similar dialogues.
  (For reproducing your own dialogues see chapter 18.)

Teaching English as a foreign language

5 Mini dialogues (sometimes called micro dialogues)
Below is a suggested way of using a mini dialogue in class:
a Give the students a picture, or suggest a situation, in which two people are talking to each other.
b Discuss with the students what is being said. List various alternatives.
c Ask the students, in pairs, to produce a simple four- to six-line dialogue to be acted out.
d When any errors have been pointed out, the students then write down or act out their dialogue.

Dialogues are fun and students learn a lot from them.

2 What to teach – the basics

Planning a lesson

1 Whether you take a class every morning or just once a week, you should plan ahead what you would like to be done in the time available. A plan gives you and your students **specific aims**.

2 The general aim of all your teaching is that students should *learn the language*. Learning the language means learning:

pronunciation
vocabulary } by practising the four skills { listening / speaking / reading / writing
grammar

If you keep these seven headings in mind when you plan your lessons, you will make sure that you are not neglecting any aspect of language learning.

The amount of practice in each of the four skills will be determined by the needs of the students. For example, much less writing is done in classes whose only aim is oral communication.

3 What to teach
Except for the first lesson of a course, all lessons should be linked in sequence and based on an overall syllabus or scheme of work. In most cases the scheme of work is closely related to a textbook, or textbooks, which provide the basis of *what* is to be learned.

4 Planning
- Your morning's teaching may be divided like this:

9.15–10.40	Low intermediate group
11.00–12.30	Advanced group

  Although you may be able to plan one activity to last the whole hour and a half for the advanced group, the lower group will need more variety – at least two activities. Each must be separately planned.

- The main thing to remember is that *students learn by being actively involved in the lesson*. They do *not* learn just by listening to you. The lesson notes that follow concentrate on **student activity**, not teacher activity. You should always aim to reduce 'teacher talking time' to a minimum.

Teaching English as a foreign language

Intermediáte   9.15 – 10.40   Room A2   Tuesday, 19 October

GRAMMAR: Past simple tense – statements and question forms

VOCABULARY (all shown on flash cards):
List 1: (a) watch television/a football match
         (b) listen to records/the radio
             play chess/tennis/football/cards
         (c) go to a film/a disco; go for a swim/a walk

List 2: (a) cook a meal; walk in the park; wash my jeans
         (b) stay at home; clean my room
             cycle round to a friend's house
         (c) eat a big meal; write a letter
             tell my baby brother a story

PRONUNCIATION: Contrast '-ed' in watched/played, etc
               (/t/; /d/)

9.15   Revision through oral questioning, or test homework orally.

9.20   Register

9.25   State main aim of lesson: To learn how to use the past simple tense of useful verbs.

       Introduce vocabulary to be used through flash cards and oral repetition.

9.30   Students practise using the vocabulary by answering questions in present simple and present continuous tenses. (Chorus and individual work/use of flash cards) E.g. What is he doing? Does she play tennis? Do you ...?
       Students ask and answer same questions in pairs. (Pair work)

9.45   Show contrast between present simple and past simple tenses in two lists headed Statement and Question. (Write lists on board or show in textbook.) Establish past time, e.g. yesterday.

9.50   Students answer questions in past simple tense. (Chorus and individual) E.g. What did she do yesterday?/ at 2 o'clock?/this morning?/last night? Did you ...?

9.55   Pair work using past simple tense.

10.00 Introduce more verbs (list 2) with similar past simple forms, through flash cards and oral repetition.

10.05 Students act out a conversation in pairs using past simple tense (model supplied).

10.15 Write vocabulary and verb forms on board/handout (or in textbook).
       Students read vocabulary and verb forms from board/textbook/handout and then copy down.

10.20 Students complete written exercise.

10.25 Proceed to a contrasting activity, e.g. a game.

10.40 Break

What to teach – the basics

5 Your own lesson notes for the intermediate lesson in the fourth week of a full-time course might look like the plan shown on page 18.

6 I have set down the lesson plan in great detail to show *exactly* what would go on. With experience your lesson notes would, of course, be much shorter, but you should always know in advance:
- the sequence of events.
- the examples and vocabulary to use.
- the questions to be asked.
- the methods (for example, pair work).
- the teaching aids (for example, flash cards).

7 In the plan on page 18 there is **variety of activity**, which keeps the students attentive and interested.

8 Being able to judge how long each part of a lesson will take comes with experience. Plans cannot be rigidly enforced because:
- unforeseen problems arise.
- some parts of the lesson are so fruitful that you decide to exploit them.

However, if you find that your lessons *never* go according to plan, something is wrong!

9 It is always worth writing down your lesson plan, even if it is only three or four lines long, because:
- it is something to refer to in times of stress or fatigue.
- after the lesson it is a record of what you have done (if you completed it – if not, plan the next lesson accordingly).

Lessons must be planned.

Vocabulary

1 Absolute beginners
a Absolute beginners learn vocabulary by **direct method** teaching – by repeating, after you, the word or phrase while you:
- point at the object.
- show a picture.
- perform the action.

and then by answering simple questions like *'What is this?'*,

'Where is the. . . ?, 'What am I doing?'

b At this very early stage it is important to follow the 'listen, speak, read, write' sequence. If you show the written word before the students are used to it orally, they are likely to get into bad pronunciation habits. You should have the whole class saying the words and phrases properly before you write the word down. Try to avoid words like *cough, through, height*.

2 General procedure for teaching vocabulary

a When you are planning your lesson (chapter 6), select the important new words and phrases.

b Explain the words carefully through clear illustration or demonstration. A lot of confusion can start at this point if your explanations are long and wordy. Methods mentioned in **1** above for basic vocabulary cannot always be used with more abstract words.

c Ask students to repeat the word or phrase, for the sound.

d Use the word in another sentence, in another context.

e Ask students to use it orally in sentences.

f Dictate it in context.

g Give the students the meaning and ask them for the word or phrase.

h Set exercises using the vocabulary.

i Ask them to write it down in their vocabulary notebooks.

All the above procedures cannot be completed in the same lesson. Learning vocabulary is a progressive activity where a lot of repetition is needed.

3 Beginners' classes can only manage to learn five to eight new words or phrases. Intermediates can manage up to 12 new words or phrases. The lesson may have more new items than this, but you select the ones you want to be learned. For beginners, select words which are useful, relevant, easily illustrated or demonstrated, and easily pronounced.

Do not expect a class to learn too many new words in one lesson.

4 The vocabulary you select should make its way into the students' **active vocabulary**, that is, the words they can understand *and produce*. Other words and phrases will, one hopes, become part of their **passive vocabulary**, that is, those they can understand

What to teach – the basics

only. (Passive vocabulary is always larger than active.)

5 Revision of vocabulary

A good textbook will do this for you, that is, it will use words introduced in one chapter again in the next and so on. However, *you* must make sure that there is revision. A good time for doing oral revision of vocabulary is at the beginning or end of a lesson.

Depending on the level of student, you can revise vocabulary by:
- showing clear pictures or drawings on the board (beginners).
- performing actions (all levels).
- writing a sentence with a blank space for the word or phrase (all levels).
- presenting a short passage or dialogue which uses the vocabulary in a slightly different context (beginners/intermediate).
- asking the students questions like,
  'What was the word (phrase) we had yesterday which meant. . . .? Now use it in a sentence please.' (Intermediate/advanced).

Vocabulary, like grammar, is learned through use.

Grammar

1 To teach the grammar (or **structure**) of English, you, the teacher, have to know it first! You must, at least, know most of it. For the rest, you need a good reference grammar book:
- to help you prepare parts of your lessons.
- for reference by your more advanced students in class.
- for *you* to refer to occasionally in class.

2 Grammar is taught in three stages:

a The teacher *presents* the grammar in one form or another.
b Students *practise* the grammar.
c Students *use* it in communication.

3 There are various ways of presenting a new grammar item. Supposing you want to teach the past perfect continuous tense. (Example: *I had been working.*) Which approach would you take?

ANALYTICAL APPROACH (deductive)
a State the name, meaning and form of the tense.

21

b Give examples of it.
c Set oral and/or written exercises on it.

PRACTICAL APPROACH

a Students read and understand a prose passage or dialogue which contains examples of the tense.
b Draw the students' attention to the examples of the tense by asking questions which can be answered only by using that tense.
c Name the tense and show how it is formed.
d Ensure that the students understand the difference in meaning between this tense and a similar one (for example, the present perfect continuous).
e Practise the tense orally in other contexts.
f Set a written exercise on it.

SITUATIONAL APPROACH

This is a variation of the practical approach.

a The teacher builds up a story or situation through pictures and questions to students. The situation must be chosen carefully so that the grammar point being taught arises naturally.
b The students add to the story or expand the situation, thus using the grammer point.

4 Most teachers find that the practical approach works best because in this way grammar is presented, not in an abstract way, but *in a context and in action*. However, the choice of approach depends ultimately on the grammar point being taught and the level of the students.

5 A good textbook, which **presents** the grammar in the way you think it ought to be presented, is obviously a great asset. However, do not be a slave to the textbook. If you think you can improve on its presentation of a particular item of grammar for your particular students, do it your own way.

6 In the **practice stage** you need a variety of oral and written exercises and drills. *One short exercise of 10 sentences or questions is quite inadequate*. Exercises done previously can quickly be revised at the beginning of the next lesson. Some grammar points need constant revision.

7 In the **communication stage**, the emphasis is on using the tense in as realistic a situation as possible. The following situation might be suggested to intermediate students as a way of using the past perfect continuous tense:

Last year a detective was investigating a fire in a private house. He wanted to know what everyone in the house *had been doing* before the fire broke out. He found out that:
(a) Mr Davis, the old man, *had been sleeping in his* room.
Now suggest what these other people had been doing:
(b) Mrs Davis, his wife, . . .
(c) Clara, their eighteen-year-old granddaughter, . . .
(d) Mark, her younger brother, . . .
(e) The gardener, . . .

8 Grammar or structure is at the heart of language and it is very important that it is learned thoroughly through *use*. No amount of learning of vocabulary or phrases can make up for a student's inability to *use the grammar correctly*.

Pronunciation

1 Firstly, we should accept the fact that, with a very few exceptions, our students *do not need perfect British accents*. Their main aim is **communication**, which means that their accent has to be good enough to be understood.

2 Different nationalities will have pronunciation difficulties with different sounds. In a mixed (multi-lingual) class, more group and individual practice is needed. In a single nationality (mono-lingual) group, you will soon discover the sounds which cause most trouble.

3 Pronunciation practice should be given in:
- **vowel sounds** (p<u>a</u>t and p<u>i</u>t)
- **consonants** (<u>b</u>at and <u>p</u>at)
- **sound clusters** (<u>streng</u>th, <u>filthy</u>)
- **word stress** (pólitics, political, politícian)
- **sentence stress** and **intonation** (see below)

4 Pronunciation practice means *listening* and *distinguishing* one

sound from another as well as *saying* the sounds properly. One way to help students to distinguish sounds is as follows:
a Write up a list of pairs of words which the students find difficult to hear as different (for example, *bell* and *pill*).
b Ask the students to copy down the words.
c Read out the words while the students listen.
d Now read out one of each pair *in random order* and ask the students to tick the word on their paper. Check them one by one.

5 Sentence stress
English is a *stress-timed* language. Longer sentences do not always take a longer time to say than shorter ones. For example:
  The <u>bus</u> was <u>late</u>.
  The number <u>three</u> bus was <u>late</u>.
  The number three bus was <u>late</u> this <u>morning</u>.
The sentences get longer but they each have only two main stressed words and all take much the same length of time to say. Most students find this a major stumbling block in pronunciation.

You should choose groups of sentences like the ones above, write them on the board, point out the stressed words and make the whole class, or groups of students, repeat the sentences at the correct speed. You may have to beat time, as if you were conducting an orchestra!

6 Intonation
Very early in their course, beginners must learn to raise or lower their voice in questions, like this:

  You're Susan, aren't you? ↗

The question tag (*aren't you?*) said with **rising intonation**, means that the speaker is really not sure whether the person is Susan or not. Compare the following:

  You're Susan, aren't you (?) ↘

With a slight fall tone, the speaker is almost certain he/she is right. It is hardly a question at all.

Students are very interested in this aspect of learning English because they *do* want to be polite. Good intonation is often the key.

What to teach – the basics

Here are another two examples:

Are you coming (?) (a polite invitation) ↗

Are you coming (?) (almost an order, or suggesting indifference) ↘

Indicate rising and falling intonation patterns both with your hands and by using arrows on the board, as in these examples.

Foreigners often appear to be rude because they have intonation problems.

3 Ways and means

Visual materials

1 An interesting picture makes a strong visual impact and gives rise to a lot of useful oral work. On the whole the students' language will be much more spontaneous and lively than when oral work is based on the written word.

2 Sources of pictures
- Learn how to draw simply on the blackboard or on your own handouts (chapter 18).
- Photocopy pictures from various sources and reproduce them (but beware copyright regulations).
- Cut out pictures from magazines.
- Use slides and photographs.
- Buy a few wallcharts.
- Choose a textbook with a good selection of pictures.
- Use an overhead projector, film and video.
- Use street maps and plans of school or college buildings.

3 The same picture can be used by classes of different levels. A beginners' class may only be able to name the objects in a room and say how many people there are. An advanced class should be able to describe the look on the people's faces, suggest what might just have happened and so on.

4 More advice on how to use pictures is given in the next section (chapter 11). In the course of your teaching you should try to build up a stock of pictures and store them so that you can easily find the ones you want. The pictures below, for example, are useful for teaching verbs of movement.

5 Be sure that your pictures are:
- clear.
- relevant to what is being taught.
- large enough to be seen by everyone in the class if this is the way you intend to use them. (Smaller pictures are ideal for group or pair work.)
- mounted on cardboard and laminated (sealed), so that they can be used again and again.

Ways and means

Using pictures

1 Small single pictures or photos
These can be used:
- to stimulate oral work in the first five minutes of a lesson until the whole class is present. For example, you give out one picture to each pair of students so that they can ask each other questions.
- to introduce the vocabulary of the lesson – how can you explain parts of a car, for instance, without pictures?
- as cues or prompts for drills (chapter 16).
- for picture lotto and other games.
- to illustrate a group of interrelated words.
- to illustrate the main stages in a narrative. Textbooks often provide illustrations, partly to explain the written text, partly to provide opportunity for oral revision. (See 'picture series' below.)

2 Picture series

These can be used as the basis for oral and written composition.

- Number each picture on the back for easy reference and because the sequence is not always clear.
- Help the lower levels of student to build up the story by indicating words through gesture, mime or a vocabulary list at the beginning of the lesson.
- Do not be surprised if your students interpret the pictures differently from you!
- Once the first student has described picture one, the next student repeats this and then adds a description of picture two and so on, thus giving built-in revision and keeping the class alert.
- If the oral composition is then to be written down, the teacher can:

    write up on the board a composite version to be copied, line by line;

    or write up some key vocabulary, phrases and structures on

the board and ask the students to write the composition
themselves;
or ask students each to provide a sentence of the narrative.
Then write up on the board, sentence by sentence.

3 Sets of pictures

These are good for building up a range of related vocabulary. You
could collect, for example, sets of pictures, one for each student, for
the following categories:

people's faces
people at work
people eating and drinking
vehicles
buildings
vegetables and fruit
kinds of clothing

The kinds of pictures used by infant school teachers teaching
children their native language can be used, but you should choose
realistic pictures. Photographs are often excellent.

Realia (real objects)

1 Students don't expect to see screwdrivers, a packet of cornflakes,
a telephone in the classroom! Their very novelty arouses attention.
If you arouse the attention of your students you have made a good
start to the lesson.

2 Realia are useful in a number of ways:
- They can be used during the first five minutes of a lesson, while latecomers are still arriving, to stimulate oral work.
- They are a very direct way of teaching vocabulary.
    This is a . . . (you show the object)
    Where is it?
    What is it used for?
- They can be handled by the students, which gives rise to a whole range of descriptive vocabulary – of shape, texture, size and so on.
- They can be used as a way of introducing a whole range of associated vocabulary (for example, screwdriver – screw – tool – DIY – . . .).

Teaching English as a foreign language

- They can be used to build up dialogues (for example, with a ticket and a programme).
- They can be used in a communicative activity as a prop (a telephone, for example). The teacher gives the phone to each student in turn and has a simple conversation with him/her; or two students take part.
- A group of objects can be used for *Kim's Game* (chapter 28).

3 The general term **realia** is often extended to mean **authentic material** of all kinds, some of which are discussed in chapter 21.

Magazine and newspaper articles, cartoons, letters from official bodies, leaflets, shopping lists, instructions for use of a machine, etc, can all be used to introduce elements of realism into a lesson. Most of this material can be used in the ways mentioned in paragraph 2 above.

4 For example, a lesson about an accident involving a car and a pedestrian can be vividly brought to life if the teacher can produce:
- a driver's licence
- a certificate of car insurance
- a blood donor's card

5 Provided that you do not use realia too often, their impact is strong. As a way of learning certain items of vocabulary, realia are unbeatable.

Recorded material

1 Your own voice is the most powerful 'teaching aid'. However, you should also use recorded speech because:
- you must let the class hear male voices if you are female and vice versa.
- your class needs to hear a *variety* of voices and accents, particularly if the class is at intermediate or advanced level.
- the class will need concentrated listening practice (chapter 14).
- recorded speech gives your own overworked voice a rest – language teaching is very tiring!
- the tape can be played many times giving exactly the same stress and intonation every time.

2 Sources of recorded speech
There are three main possibilities:
- record the voices of your friends, family, colleagues.
- record programmes direct from radio or TV (where copyright allows).
- buy the commercially produced tapes which often go with textbooks (good tapes have sound effects for extra realism).

3 Using the cassette recorder in class
The cassette/tape recorder can be used for:
- recording and playing back the students' own voices.
- playing dialogues (chapter 5).
- playing drills (chapter 16).
- giving listening comprehension exercises (chapter 14).
- playing sounds and songs.
- giving pronunciation exercises – however often recorded speech is played, the *pronunciation never changes*.

4 The most useful type of machine has:
- battery and mains input.
- a rev counter (to find your place on the tape).
- an extra hand microphone on a long flex with a stop/go button (and a solid state microphone).
- a re-cap button.

5 You should have your own machine.
- Relying on being able to borrow one belonging to the school or to someone else is far too risky.
- There are several types of recorder and knowing your own machine is a great advantage.
- You can have the recording ready before you come into the classroom.
- You can have it when you want for spontaneous, unplanned use.

6 Practical advice
- Before you play a tape to the students, make sure you know what it sounds like, at the correct volume, *in the classroom*. A tape which sounds all right in your own home may not be clear enough or loud enough in a classroom.
- Place the recorder where all students will hear it clearly.

Ways and means

- Place the recorder on a surface which does not vibrate.
- Keep the tapes and recorder free of dust.
- Have a note of the number on the rev counter of where the recordings start.

7 Video tapes

Commercially produced video tapes can be a powerful stimulus to oral work. One type of recording for language work is of a conversation between two or three people, against the authentic background of the country – people buying food in a market, for example.

With this type of recording, the teacher can proceed as follows:
a Briefly introduce the content and vocabulary of the recording.
b Play the whole video tape.
c Ask simple questions about it.
d Play it again, in sections if it is longer than three minutes.
e Ask more detailed questions, perhaps introducing a point of grammar usage.
f Play the tape *without the sound*, asking students to provide the language or to describe generally what is going on.
g Use the vocabulary, pronunciation and grammar in a variety of exercises – oral and/or written.
h At the end of the lesson, play the whole video tape again, sound and vision.

Although video tapes are of great value as far as language is concerned, they also provide the atmosphere and visual background of the country.

Practice in listening

1 When you talk to the class, the students are (you hope!) listening and trying to understand you. The fact that they are able to *see* you, in particular your facial expressions and gestures, helps them to understand what you are saying.

If, however, you play a recording on a tape, the students have to listen much more carefully. They are listening *without the help of visual clues*. Exercises to practise this are called **listening comprehension** exercises.

Teaching English as a foreign language

2 The normal procedure for listening comprehension is as follows:
a Introduce the students to the *content* and *vocabulary* of what they are about to hear.
b Set the rev counter at zero so that you can easily find the beginning again.
c Play the tape (in sections with lower levels of students, noting the rev counter numbers).
d Give questions or instructions, oral or written, to test the students' comprehension (after each section in some cases). These questions must be prepared before you give the lesson.
e Set a time limit for the completion of the exercise, if it is written.
f Play the tape again.

The tape may be played a third time (depending on the difficulty or length). If the students are working in a language laboratory, they can play the tape back at will.

3 Testing listening comprehension
Nearly all forms of testing listening comprehension involve the students' other language skills (speaking, reading or writing). It is therefore important that whenever you set a test you and the students should know *what* is being tested (chapter 26).

The only way of testing listening comprehension and no other skill, is to pre-record a set of instructions and *watch* the student carrying out these instructions in a physical way. This can be done as follows: Tell the student to listen carefully to the tape and do what he/she is asked to do. Then play the pre-recorded tape which says, for example:

Stand behind the desk.
Open the drawer with your right hand.
Take out the white envelope.
Put it under the pair of scissors on the desk.
Now close the drawer.
You are going to make a telephone call.
Pick up the receiver.
Dial 01-328-5716.
That was 01-328-5716, etc.

This type of exercise is a little artificial. However, many real life situations require the skill of listening to and understanding instructions (for example, driving lessons, telephone answering machines). By setting the exercise in such a context, practice will be of relevance to the students.

4 The value of listening comprehension is that, without visual clues, the listener's ear becomes more receptive and acute. Initially, it is very hard work for the student, who may protest that he/she cannot understand anything. Give your students a lot of help (by constantly replaying short sections, giving vocabulary clues and visual clues), so that their confidence grows.

Language laboratories

1 Language laboratories are designed to give students **concentrated individual oral practice** in the language they are learning. Wearing headphones with a microphone attached, students work individually, doing the following:

- listening to the tape or teacher } **audio-active**
- repeating or responding (replying) } **laboratories**

The above functions, plus

- recording their own voice } **audio-comparative**
- playing back recordings   } **laboratories** (i.e.
- talking to the teacher   } those with a tape recorder for each student)

2 Language laboratories are particularly good for **drills** (chapter 16) and for **listening comprehension** (chapter 14). Although they give concentrated oral practice, *they do not give practice in real communication* (face to face talking), because the machine 'gets in the way'.

3 A language laboratory is a **teaching aid**, not a complete teaching system. It will help students learn if the teacher knows how and when to use it. One of the most common mistakes made by teachers is to expect students to keep the headphones on for too long. Listening and 'replying' to a machine is tiring, so a lesson in the laboratory should be broken up. For example, an hour's session with an intermediate group could be arranged like this:

Teaching English as a foreign language

Activity	Time (in minutes)	Use of laboratory
1 Teacher introduces dialogue and teaches new vocabulary	5	—
2 Students hear dialogue	10	✓
3 Students repeat (parts of) dialogue		
4 Pronunciation drills (based on dialogue)	5	✓
5 Explanation of grammar points	10	—
6 Grammar drills	5	✓
7 Written exercises based on above	10	—
8 Oral comprehension questions	10	✓

4 The above session introduces some new material, but the laboratory is more often used for **consolidation**, **revision** or **testing**. Below is an example of a half-hour's session with good beginners. In a previous classroom session, the students have already read and understood the episode of the story they are about to hear.

Activity	Time (in minutes)	Use of laboratory
1 Students listen to story	3	✓
2 Students answer comprehension questions	10	✓
3 Students listen to and repeat 15 words from the story for pronunciation practice.	3	✓
4 Teacher writes up the words on the board. Students copy the words into notebooks.	4	—
5 Students listen to and repeat whole sentences (from the story) containing the words.	10	✓

5 Language laboratories with individual tape recorders (audio-comparative) also provide excellent private study facilities. A school which can afford even a few language laboratory units can offer the keen student hours of extra practice in the language.

6 Language laboratories have to be looked after and maintained in good working order by a person with technical ability. Good laboratories are manufactured by TANDBERG.
Working with a laboratory needs practice. Do not expect to become an expert overnight!

Drills

1 A drill is a means of providing intensive practice of grammatical structure, word order or pronunciation. The best drills are those which make students think before they reply; the worst are those which need only a mechanical response.

2 Example of a mechanical drill
TEACHER: Did he go out last night?
STUDENT: Yes, he did.
TEACHER: Did she see him yesterday?
STUDENT: Yes, she did.
TEACHER: Did Julie get the job?
STUDENT: Yes, she did.
TEACHER: Did the boys buy the food?
STUDENT: Yes, they did.

3 Example of a more useful and interesting drill
Aim: To practise the past simple tense. (Student to choose the item either according to information already given or at random.)
TEACHER: Did she buy the bread at the supermarket or at the bakers?
STUDENT: She bought it at the_____.
TEACHER: Did he teach mathematics or languages?
STUDENT: He taught_____.
TEACHER: Did they go to the pictures or to the theatre?
STUDENT: They went to the_____.
TEACHER: Did Susan give £500 or £600 for the car?
STUDENT: She gave_____.

4 Example of a stress and intonation drill
Aim: To practise questioning a statement.
TEACHER: John's coming.
STUDENT: <u>Is</u> John coming?

TEACHER: They've finished.
STUDENT: Have they finished?
TEACHER: They're getting married.
STUDENT: Are they getting married?

The student could be asked to add '*I can't believe it!*' to each reply.

5 If the above drills are done in class by the teacher, each question or cue is probably asked twice, with a second student answering the second time. There should be about 8 to 10 questions or cues in a drill.

6 Drills in the language laboratory

Taped drills are often three- or four-phase:

PHASE 1 (MASTER RECORDING): I think Peter will come.
PHASE 2 (STUDENT): Well, he hasn't come yet.
PHASE 3 (MASTER): Well, he hasn't come yet.
(PHASE 4 (STUDENT): Well, he hasn't come yet.)

Phases 1 and 3 are recorded on the tape so that they cannot be erased by the student. Phase 2 (and 4, if required) are gaps on the tape to be recorded by the student.

The gaps must be of the right length. If they are too short, the student cannot respond properly and soon gives up. If they are too long, the student either begins to relax and lose interest or to give a longer response than necessary.

7 Laboratory drills are useful because:
- the teacher's voice is rested.
- the teacher can concentrate on listening to the students one by one.
- a variety of voices and accents can be introduced.
- in an audio-comparative laboratory (chapter 15) the students can perfect the drill working at their own speed.

Textbooks

1 There is a wide range of textbooks in teaching English as a foreign or second language. Often the textbook is chosen for the class teacher by the Director of Studies or Head of Department, but if you are asked to choose your own, take plenty of time and care in doing this. You will be rewarded by having to do less preparation yourself during the course.

2 You should work with a textbook which follows the kind of syllabus or approach that you prefer. There are three main kinds of approach:

STRUCTURAL
A structurally-based textbook is characterized by the careful build-up of grammar in a planned sequence. Details of each chapter, on the contents page, tend to reflect this.

SITUATIONAL
Chapters tend to be entitled 'At the station', 'At the hairdresser's' and so on. The main emphasis is the building up of a range of useful vocabulary and grammar connected with a selection of everyday situations.

NOTIONAL – FUNCTIONAL
(sometimes referred to simply as functional)
This is a more recent approach and is not always suitable for beginners. Each chapter or unit deals with a **function** of language like 'asking', 'persuading', 'arguing' and so on, and is based on several situations where this function is required. For example:
persuading your friend to go out to a disco
asking for information at a tourist office

3 Of course there is no reason why a class should not have access to more than one textbook. In fact it is unlikely that all the work you want the students to do will be covered in one textbook. Listening comprehension (chapter 14) and composition writing (chapter 24), for example, often require another text, particularly with good intermediate students.

4 Checklist for choosing a textbook
- syllabus/approach
- layout and size
- good pictures
- tapes available
- balance of skills (speaking, listening, reading, writing)
- vocabulary index
- grammatical index
- revision

- useful teacher's book
- suitability of content
- examination or non-examination orientated
- price

5 A good textbook, suited to the students' interests and needs, is a major asset to the course. Working systematically through it, students can see the progress they are making and can easily revise what they have done.

Handouts and worksheets

1 If you have access to a spirit duplicator (also called a banda machine) and a good supply of run-off paper, you can quickly make inexpensive copies of exercises, drills, maps, diagrams, pictures and so on – anything that you can draw or write yourself on the master sheet. Photocopiers are more efficient but more expensive.

2 **Worksheets** have spaces in which your students can fill in their answers. They are excellent for homework questions, because marking is much quicker and easier when questions and answers are on the same sheet.

3 **Handouts** are sheets of information to be used:
- as references (for example, lists of the three different pronunciations of past participles ending in -ed).
- as the basis for an exercise (for example, a map or an extract from a train timetable).
- as the correct version of an exercise (for example, a dictation), so that the students can mark their own.
- as a scheme of work (for example, a list of compositions to be written with the dates when they are to be handed in).

4 **Presentation**
- On a worksheet spacing is very important. If students are to write in the gaps, or to complete two or three lines of writing, you must allow for a wide variation in size of writing.
- Messy handouts and worksheets – like messy writing on the blackboard – encourage messy work from students.

Your writing must be absolutely clear, much clearer than you would make it for native speakers.

5 Your students will appreciate your handouts and worksheets because they know that they have been made specifically for them.

Prose passages
(Descriptive, discursive or narrative passages written in ordinary prose form.)

Faced with a prose passage in the textbook, how do you proceed? Don't just open the book and ask one student to start reading! The first priority for the student is to *understand* the passage. To ensure that this happens, some preparation is required.

1 Reading and comprehension
a Introduce the passage in a way which *arouses the students' interest* (any methods are acceptable). Do this *before* the students look at the passage.

b Explain some of the new vocabulary (chapter 7) and write it on the board. Select only **key** items, that is, words which are essential to the understanding of the text.

c Encourage students to *predict* what they will read and to share their knowledge of the subject.

d Write a few general questions on the board. The answers to these should provide the main gist of the passage.

e Ask students to read the passage silently to themselves and to look for the answers to the questions in **d**.

f Elicit answers from the students. Go round the class hearing several students' answers to each question, before saying whether they are correct.

g Ask further comprehension questions either orally or on handouts for students to work on in groups or pairs. If the latter, make sure you bring students back into a single group to decide on the correct answers.

h In order to check understanding of vocabulary, use the methods suggested in chapter 7, but particularly try giving the meaning and asking for the word. For example, 'Which word in the passage means *to walk slowly?*'

i If the passage has really aroused the students' interest, a discussion should follow on quite naturally.

2 Reading aloud and pronunciation

Instead of asking students to read a passage silently, you could ask them to read it aloud. Some teachers, however, believe this is an artificial and unrealistic exercise.

a Read aloud a whole paragraph yourself before you ask students to read it. (*You* give the model pronunciation.)

b Ask each student to read aloud a few sentences only, never a whole paragraph. (Nothing bores a class more quickly than to have to listen to another student struggle through reading.)

c The whole of a long passage need not be read out aloud, but some work should be given on all of it.

When the passage is being read aloud, or when questions are being answered, several pronunciation difficulties (chapter 9) will have come to light. You may have dealt with them as you went along, but at the end you should choose three or four difficult words, phrases or sentences and organize some pronunciation practice on them.

3 Grammar

Prose passages in textbooks are usually written so that they illustrate certain grammatical constructions. When you are sure that the passage has been understood and that the class is fairly confident orally with the new vocabulary, you should highlight the main grammar (chapter 8).

You then proceed to do the exercises (the ones that *you* have decided to do, not necessarily every single exercise).

4 Most of the above advice is particularly relevant to good beginners up to good intermediate classes. More advanced classes may need to tackle a prose passage in different ways – less help from the teacher, more dictionary work by the student and so on. Prose passages at advanced level often lead on to **summaries** and **essays**.

Extensive reading

There are two ways of reading, intensively and extensively.

1 Intensive reading

Students reading **intensively** look at every word, take notice of punctuation, sentences and paragraphs, understand the grammar and so on. Intensive reading often becomes an exercise in recognizing the rules of the English language in action. Beginners and low intermediate groups tend to read intensively.

Most textbook reading has, until recently, been intensive. The reading of written instructions, recipes, application forms and so on is necessarily intensive.

2 Extensive reading

The aim here is to get on with the story, to *read for gist*, not detail, and to read much more quickly.

Extensive reading should give good students some of the pleasure they have when reading novels in their own language (if they read novels). It should submerge them in the foreign language. It is important to find good reading material which *interests* the students and makes them *want to read on*.

3 Motivation

Extensive reading is highly motivating! Once students have become used to it, they enjoy it because:
- it is an individual activity, which frees the student from the restrictions of classwork.
- students read at their own pace.
- they can choose what they read.

4 Fact or fiction?

Whatever you may prefer your students to read, their wishes and interests should be respected. You need to keep a good variety of books in the classroom, and there should also be easy access to a library.

There is a growing number of easy readers produced especially for the EFL/ESL market. I would also recommend, for both fact and fiction, the *Ladybird* series – the vast choice is enough to keep a whole intermediate class reading for a year.

At later levels, students should be encouraged to read magazines and newspapers. For earlier levels, these can be adapted or rewritten to suit the level of the students (see also chapter 21).

5 Keeping a record
You or the students should keep a record of what each student has read. Some extensive reading may form the basis of composition writing, but the main idea of extensive reading is *pleasure and interest in reading*.

Authentic material

1 It is easy, in the UK, to obtain authentic reading and listening matter (that is not 'textbook' English) for good intermediate and advanced classes. This same material can be used equally well with lower levels, provided the *tasks* (or exercises) you set are graded according to the level of the class.

2 Pamphlets and brochures
Collect the required number of free copies of various publicity material from a variety of sources, for example:
>banks and building societies
>local library
>travel agents
>British Rail travel offices
>local tourist information centres
>Citizens Advice Bureaux

Your students will take a great interest in this material because they know that the English used is not 'textbook stuff' but the genuine article.

3 Suggested sequence of a lesson using a set of pamphlets/brochures with a class
a Orally introduce the subject matter. There may be some brief discussion at this point.
b Write one or two key words, facts, or ideas on the board.
c Give out the pamphlets, one to each student (or pair of students in a large class).
d Ask the students to look through it rapidly (looking at layout, headings, main sections).
e Ask students to state briefly what the pamphlet is about.
f Read and discuss with them one or two sections in detail.
g Read and discuss the rest of the main headings or items.

h Set homework based on the pamphlet (for example, comprehension questions, a summary, an essay).
i Follow up the homework as necessary.
A practical point. If you set comprehension questions, number and mark or underline the answer in your own copy of the pamphlet, so that marking is easier when the homework comes in.

A similar sequence can be followed, using a tape of authentic *listening* material.

4 Newspapers
A few newspapers will provide a wealth of topical material for a class of advanced students. Specific articles can be read and discussed in much the same way as outlined in section 3 above.

In addition, pairs of students can be asked to select items from the paper which most interests them, and to report on these to the rest of the class.

Some **magazines** can also be used in this way.

5 Authentic material outside the UK
It is more difficult to obtain sets of authentic material outside the UK. You probably have to rely on single copies, which means that the work done on them is likely to be individual or pair work.

The suggested procedure in section 3 above will have to be modified so that instead of a class lesson, the students refer to instructions on 'work cards' which tell them how to proceed. When they have completed the work, they can report back to the teacher or to the class.

6 Reading and listening to authentic material improves the students' range of vocabulary and also gives them glimpses of the way of life in Britain. For example, intermediate students can learn a lot from a lesson based on a holiday brochure produced by Butlins.

Specific grammar points often emerge naturally from study of authentic material, for example, the use of *imperatives* in holiday brochures and the use of the *present simple tense* in instruction leaflets.

Dictation

1 When we give our students a dictation we hope that they will show proof of:
- a trained ear
- ability to spell
- knowledge of grammar
- ability to grasp context.

2 It is arguable that if the course is aiming at oral fluency (and not written competence), dictations are irrelevant, being little more than a spelling test in disguise.

However, dictations (which need not be long and difficult) do test more than spelling. You can dictate:
- lists of words
- pairs of words
- a few sentences or a short paragraph.

3 A useful distinction can be made between a **test dictation** and a **practice dictation**.

PRACTICE DICTATION
The students have been studying a passage or a dialogue and you ask them to close the book. You then *either* give a dictation based on it *or* dictate parts of it word for word. In both cases your students are *consolidating what they know*. You or the students can mark the dictation, but it should be marked and corrected immediately.

TEST DICTATION
This is *not* part of the learning process but an *assessment*. You give the students an unseen dictation of a standard you think they should be able to cope with. You mark it yourself and the results can be used either to tell you how effective your teaching has been or as a guide to the students' ability (diagnostic).

4 The usual procedure for a longer dictation is:
a read the whole passage while students listen only.
b dictate each short section, pause, and repeat each section.
c read the passage again without pauses.
d allow a minute or two for final checking.

5 If you think that dictating prose passages or dialogues is an artificial exercise, you could dictate a memorandum or a letter, since these are authentic activities.

Short dictations given regularly do more good than occasional long ones.

Writing (up to intermediate level)

1 Writing practice for absolute beginners consists of getting used to English script and, for some nationalities, to the way we write from left to right and from top to bottom of the page. At this early stage straightforward copying exercises are necessary.

2 Up to low intermediate level, the writing needs to be fairly controlled:
- copying phrases and sentences which have been mastered orally.
- constructing sentences partly or wholly from a grid or substitution table:

While	I he she	was	walking going driving cycling	to	the cinema, the cafe, the disco, school, church,	I he . . . she

- constructing sentences from a few given words:
  We / film / tonight
  You / my house / tomorrow?
  They / London / week
- dictation of familiar sentences (see chapter 22).
- answering straightforward comprehension questions.
- reproducing from memory a short simple narrative or description practised orally in class.
- completing a dialogue (between two people, where what one person says is already given).

3 Long before students are given compositions to write (see chapter

24), they should be given practice in a variety of well prepared shorter tasks:
   personal letters
   dialogues
   instructions
   descriptions
   extracts from personal diaries

They should all be well prepared which means:
- talking about the subject matter in class.
- supplying useful vocabulary.
- revising appropriate grammatical structures.
- revising the rules of written English, for example, punctuation, spelling.
- providing, where possible, stimulus material:
   a letter to reply to
   the 'bare bones' of a narrative
   a situation for a dialogue
   a picture or picture series
- providing a model text.

Never let students complain that they have nothing to write about.

4 There is no point giving a lot of written work to students who have come on a course to improve their ability to speak, but this does not mean that writing is irrelevant to an orally based course. For most students the act of writing down vocabulary and short sentences is *visual confirmation* of what they have heard and said, a tangible record of what they have learned.

Post-intermediate writing – composition

1 At this level, composition (essay) work can be given regularly as homework to classes preparing for exams in which composition is set. Composition writing is a demanding and, some people would say, artificial exercise which needs practice and preparation. In order to write a good composition the students need:
- general language skills at the appropriate level.
- specific composition-writing skills.
- stimulus material for each composition.

2 General language skills

Students must know:
- the basic grammar and vocabulary.
- how to connect sentences.
- how to vary sentence construction.
- how to use punctuation. (Avoid teaching colons and semi-colons.)

3 Specific composition-writing skills

Students must know:
- vocabulary and phrases needed to develop
  (i) an argument: *on the other hand, as far as . . . is concerned, it is undeniable that*
  and
  (ii) a narrative: *meanwhile, shortly after, no sooner had, in the end, before doing, after doing*.
- how to plan a composition:
  writing an introduction
  constructing a paragraph
  writing a conclusion

4 Stimulus material for each composition

In order to *write* at this level the students should first *read*:
  the beginning of a story to be developed,
or an article about the subject,
or one side of the argument to be discussed.

In this way they will be introduced to relevant vocabulary. They should also have access to a good learner's dictionary – a dictionary entirely in English designed for students learning English.

5 If the word 'composition' is interpreted more freely to include dialogues, letters, speeches, articles, reports, business letters and so on, students need to be shown examples of *different styles* so that they can choose the appropriate one. For example:
  conversational
  business phraseology
  objective report
  semi-formal (speeches)
  journalistic

6 For the correction of compositions, see chapter 25.

Compositions must be well prepared.

Marking written work

1 Marking is a chore which few teachers enjoy. You can reduce marking in a number of ways:
- Prepare the students thoroughly for written work.
- Make sure that they know exactly what they have to do, for example, homework instructions should be *written*, not verbal.
- Make sure that your students have a good dictionary to refer to and know how to use it.
- Ask your students to write on alternate lines, so that you and they have space to make corrections in the blank lines.
- Tell them to read over the work carefully before handing it in – i.e. insist on high standards.
- If most of the students have made mistakes, accept the fact that *you* are to blame for bad preparation and mark selectively – i.e. don't mark every single mistake.
- Indicate errors clearly so that no time is wasted by the student trying to understand your red biro. Some teachers like to use an easy code: SP=spelling, G=grammar, for example. Others prefer to underline grammar and vocabulary mistakes and to cross out spelling mistakes. Some teachers like to show the degree of mistake by underlining one, two or three times.
- Write in the correct version only when you know that the students will be unable to correct the mistake themselves.
- Award marks regularly but not for all written work.
- Written work can often be checked by the students themselves. It is better to ask them to do this than to take in work when you are unable to mark it for the next lesson.

2 Mistakes in spelling are sometimes due to the student's poor pronunciation. For example, Spaniards may write *e*station; Arabs *bat* instead of *pet*, and so on. Grammatical mistakes may be due to interference from the student's mother tongue. The more that is known about the cause of the mistake, the more likely it is to be avoided.

3 Insist that corrections are done as soon as written work has been handed back.

4 Keep a record of the students' marks and, in the last six months before an external exam, write down exactly what the marks are for, so that weaknesses in any area can be spotted and worked on.

Testing

1 Testing your students can be informal or formal. It can be done for diagnostic purposes at the beginning of a course, or as a means of checking progress.

Informal testing is an integral part of teaching, for example:
- oral question and answer
- asking a student to repeat or explain
- giving a written 'slip test', i.e.:
  The teacher asks 10–20 quick questions.
  Students must mark their own or each other's answers.
  The results may be given orally but they are not recorded.
  The *students* know what they still have to learn.

Formal tests are usually given to students:
- at the beginning of a course to sort them into groups.
- during the course to assess progress.
- at the end of the course for a certificate or an external examination.

2 When you give your students a *formal test*:
- decide exactly what you want to test and make up questions which test that and very little else.
- make all your questions clear and unambiguous.
- tell the students how the marks are to be awarded.
- arrange the test so that it is easily, quickly and objectively marked.
- give out the results as soon as possible.

3 Formal testing can be done in various ways:

OBJECTIVE TESTS (multiple-choice tests)
- Three, four or five possible answers are given for each question.
- The student selects one.

- His/her answer is therefore 100% right or 100% wrong.
- These tests are difficult to make up but very quick to mark.
- They can test almost every aspect of a student's knowledge of English except free writing skills.

CLOZE TESTS

A prose passage is written with every seventh word missing (sometimes this pattern is not strictly followed). The student has to think of a word which fits the context. Usually only one word is possible. A carefully designed cloze test is a very searching assessment of a student's knowledge of English.

ORAL TESTS

The examiner should not award an overall *impression* mark for an oral test, but *separate* marks for some or all of the following (depending on the level of student):

For reading aloud (see chapter 9):
- pronunciation of vowels and consonants and clusters.
- intonation and stress.
- phrasing and fluency.

In an oral conversation:

The points above *and*
- quickness to respond.
- clarity of communication.

Students need to be tested so that they, and you, know what progress they are making.

Preparing for an external examination

1 The teacher needs to be able to consult a copy of:
- the current syllabus and regulations.
- the latest examiners' report.
- the exam papers of the last few years (unless the syllabus has changed).

2 Success in an examination depends on a combination of knowledge, technique and confidence.
- *Knowledge* comes from systematic and regular learning of items in the syllabus. In English this means practice in the four skills of listening, speaking, reading and writing.

- *Technique* comes from regular practice in answering exam questions in the way examiners expect them to be answered.
- *Confidence* comes from successful practice under test conditions and from a confident teacher, who should ensure that revision is carefully planned.

3 Very few students enjoy examinations and we should do as much as we can to prepare them for the 'ordeal'. A practice examination in conditions as realistic as possible is a necessary part of good preparation.

4 A list of the main examination boards in English as a Foreign Language is given in the appendix but some details of the most well-known board are given below:

CAMBRIDGE LOCAL EXAMINATIONS are held in June and December in the UK and abroad at 3 levels:
First Certificate
Certificate of Proficiency
Diploma of English Studies
For further details contact the British Council or write direct to:
The Secretary (Examinations in English),
Syndicate Buildings,
17 Harvey Road,
CAMBRIDGE CB1 2EU,
England.

Games and songs

1 Games

Games are associated in people's minds with fun and relaxation, so the chance to play a game in class is welcomed by most students. If while they are having fun and relaxing they can also be *learning* English, you are on a winning streak!

Many games involve concentration, repetition and a good memory – three good ingredients for learning. Three games are mentioned below, but see appendix 3 for some useful book titles.

KIM'S GAME (any level of student)
Take a collection of up to twenty small objects (realia) which the whole class knows the English for (taught in previous lessons).

Show the objects laid on a tray for about five minutes, then cover them and ask the students how many items they remember. This can be done orally (in teams or individually) or as a written activity.

PICTURE LOTTO (beginners or low intermediates)
'Bingo' with pictures instead of numbers.

'I WENT ON MY HOLIDAY AND IN MY SUITCASE I PACKED . . .'
The first student says the above and chooses an article. The second student repeats the above, then the first article, then a second article of his or her own choice. And so on, as the list gets longer and longer. Students making mistakes drop out. Students sit in circles of no more than 10.

2 Songs

You do not need to be a good singer yourself to introduce songs into your lessons. You can write out or say the words, and hum the tune. Better still, use songs recorded on tape. Songs prepared specially for EFL students are available commercially.

Often the tune is known by some of the students and sometimes you are lucky enough to have a student who plays the guitar.

Songs often provide good pronunciation practice and unconscious repetition of useful words and phrases. Students often want to know the words of English pop songs, and to study these in class can be highly motivating.

Singing produces a lot of laughter and enjoyment, so we should all introduce songs in the classroom from time to time.
Two possible methods of using songs in class are:

A SONG THAT STUDENTS DO NOT KNOW

a Tell students briefly what the song is about.
b Play or hum the tune (without the words).
c Sing or play a tape recording of the first two lines. Pictures on the board or flashcards can form prompts for each line.
d Ask students to repeat, several times. Sing with them!
e Play lines 3 and 4. Students repeat.
f Play lines 1 to 4 again. Students repeat.
g Proceed to teach the rest of the song more quickly.
h Finally, let them see the words. Explain where necessary, but not in great detail.

i The class sings the complete song, eventually without looking at the words.

As an alternative to **h**, give students the words in the form of a cloze test (see chapter 26). Students listen again to the song and fill in the missing words.

A POP SONG MOST OF THE STUDENTS HAVE HEARD
a Play a tape recording of the song.
b Let the students study the words.
c Play the song again. } (possibly in sections)
d Practise the song three or four lines at a time, building up to the complete song.

Songs need not be complicated. For example, at Easter we can teach 'Hot Cross Buns':

Hot cross buns!   Hot cross buns!

One a pen-ny, two a pen-ny, hot cross buns!

Songs can also be used:
- as a basis for discussion work.
- to revise specific grammar points (e.g., 'If I were a rich man', 'When I'm 64').
- as an introduction to British music styles – folk, jazz, pop and so on.

Discussions

1 Good intermediate and advanced students benefit most from discussions in English. If you decide to hold a discussion (of 15

minutes or more) in class, you should *prepare thoroughly first*:
- precede the discussion with a talk, film, visit or the study of some information so that it will be an *informed* discussion, not just idle chat.
- revise the kind of vocabulary and phrases used in discussion (for example, *in my opinion/I entirely disagree with . . .*). A list of such phrases could be written on the board.
- *choose the subject with care.* You should not expect students to discuss a subject which is likely to provoke *strong* religious or political views. In a multilingual group such a discussion may end in disaster.

As in many other classroom activities, it is wise to know your students and to respect their individuality and opinions.

2 Organization of the discussion session
- In a larger class, divide the students into two groups and seat them appropriately (see chapter 2).
- Choose a student with a good grasp of the language, but who is not domineering, to chair each group.
- Listen in on each group and answer any questions they wish to ask you, but do not interfere.
- If necessary, ask students some leading questions to stimulate discussion.
- Ask each chairperson to report back at the end of the discussion.
- Your role as teacher is to try and draw some conclusions.
- Follow up the discussion by some written work *but* if this becomes a regular chore, the students will soon lose their enthusiasm for discussions. Try to make the written task *relevant* and *realistic*.

Outings

1 An outing has to be reasonably well organized to be enjoyable. If you can also manage some educational planning, the outing should be an even greater success.

2 Before the outing
- Give the class information about it well in advance.

- Tell the class *why* they are going on the outing.
- Give them relevant vocabulary.
- Set them a few specific tasks (oral or written). For example:
  (i) to answer a number of factual questions, mainly by observation, *or* to verify whether certain statements are right or wrong.
  (ii) to describe the journey.
  (iii) to draw and label a diagram or map connected with the outing.
  (iv) to ask set questions (but each student must ask *different* questions so that staff do not have to answer the same questions over and over again).
  (v) to tape record a short conversation with one of the organizers of the visit.

A well constructed worksheet (see chapter 18) will often provide a reasonable amount of written work. Do not give too much.

3 During the outing
Enjoy youself and don't lose any students!

4 After the outing
- ALL LEVELS OF STUDENTS: Let them talk about their experiences – good or bad.
- BEGINNERS and LOW INTERMEDIATE: Ask them to do a short oral or written exercise based on the outing.
- MORE ADVANCED STUDENTS: Ask them to write a report or a composition *or* suggest reading matter connected with the outing.

5 On an outing you will learn a lot more about your students. After each successful venture the atmosphere in class improves. (The students have also learned more about you!)

Appendix 1

Examination boards

University of Cambridge Examinations Syndicate, Syndicate Buildings, 17 Harvey Road, Cambridge CB1 2EU, England.
3 levels of examination: First Certificate, Certificate of Proficiency, Cambridge Diploma.

ARELS Examination Trust, 113 Banbury Road, Oxford OX2 6JX, England.
3 levels of examination (oral only): Preliminary, Certificate, Diploma.

Oxford Delegacy of Local Examinations, Ewert Place, Summertown, Oxford OX2 7BZ, England.
2 levels of examination (reading and writing tests designed to complement the ARELS oral): Preliminary, Higher.

Royal Society of Arts Examinations Board, 8 John Adam Street, London WC2N 6AJ, England.
3 levels of examination (communicative): Basic, Intermediate, Advanced.

Joint Matriculation Board (test in English-overseas), Manchester M15 6EU, England.
1 level (intended for students wanting to study in Britain).

TOEFL
Information can be obtained from any United States embassy or consular section; or (i) for non-graduates: Test of English as a Foreign Language, Box 899, Princeton, New Jersey 08540, USA; (ii) for graduates: The Graduate Record Examinations Educational Testing Service, Box 955, Princeton, New Jersey 08540, USA; (iii) for graduates: The Graduate Management Admission Test, Educational Testing Service, Box 966, Princeton, New Jersey 08540, USA.
1 level (intended for students wanting to study in the USA).

Pitman Examination Institute, Godalming, Surrey GU7 1UV, England.
4 levels: Elementary, Intermediate, Higher Intermediate, Advanced.

Institute of Linguists, Mangold House, 24A Highbury Grove, London N5 2EA, England.
5 levels: Preliminary Certificate, Grade 1, Grade 2, Intermediate Diploma, Final Diploma.

Teaching English as a foreign language

Further details are in an annual publication called *Where to learn English in Great Britain*, published by Truman and Knightley, 76–78 Notting Hill Gate, London W11 3LJ, England. The following publication is also recommended: *The Pitman Guide to English Language Examinations for Overseas Candidates*, published by Pitman (1981).

Appendix 2

Teacher training for English language teachers

The most well-known qualifications are those certificated by the *Royal Society of Arts*, 8 John Adam Street, London WC2N 6AJ, England.
The certificates can be obtained at two levels: Preparatory and Full. One of them is designed especially for non-native speakers of English. Full details are obtainable from the Board.

Trinity College, London, offers the qualification of Licentiate Diploma for Teachers of English as a Foreign or Second Language. Information can be obtained from Trinity College, Mandeville Place, London W1M 6AQ, England.

One of the most well-known private organizations, which runs courses in EFL, also provides its own teacher training: *International House*, 106 Piccadilly, London W1V 9FL, England.

One of the most famous names in language teaching is *Berlitz*. Their headquarters are at 321 Oxford Street, London W1, England.

Appendix 3

Some recommended books

So You Want to Learn a Language by Stork. Faber (1976).
   An excellent book for adult students and teachers; short, readable and full of interesting insights.
Second Language Learning and Teaching by D. A. Wilkins. Edward Arnold (1974).
   A concise discussion of the theory and practice of teaching a second language.
Better English Pronunciation by J. D. O'Connor. Cambridge University Press (Second Edition 1980).
   A standard work on pronunciation.
Ship or Sheep? by Ann Baker. Cambridge University Press (New Edition 1981).
   An informative and entertaining introduction to English pronunciation. Highlights the pronunciation difficulties of various nationalities.
Teaching Oral English by Donn Byrne. Longman (1976).
   A good standard text on the subject.
A Practical English Grammar by Thomson and Martinet. Oxford University Press (Third Edition 1980).
   A reference grammar for you and your more advanced students.
Visual Materials for the Language Teacher by A. Wright. Longman (1976).
   Full of ideas about how to make, find and use pictures of all sizes.
The Language Laboratory and Language Learning by J. Dakin. Longman (1973).
   Good explanation of language learning theory and very practical sections on drill in the laboratory and on how to use the laboratory properly.
Games for Language Learning by Wright, Betteridge and Buckby. Cambridge University Press (1979).
Take 5 by M. Carrier. Harrap (1980).
   A collection of language games, puzzles and activities.

Appendix

ELT Guide 1: Communication Games by D. Byrne and S. Rixon. The British Council (1979).

English for Specific Purposes. The British Council (1978).
  Deals with, e.g., English for Scientists, English for Managers.

A Skeleton in the Cupboard by N. Tucker. Puffin (1979).
  A very wittily illustrated booklet of English proverbs.

How to face a class by C. Dawson. Harrap (1981).
  A short, readable and highly practical book on how to teach.

The English Teacher's Handbook by R. V. White. Harrap (1982).
  An introduction to English Language Teaching; describes traditional approaches as well as more recent developments.

Oxford Advanced Learner's Dictionary of Current English by A. S. Hornby. Oxford University Press (Third Edition 1974).
  Gives practical definitions in simple English.

Practical English Teaching (PET).
  An excellent magazine available from Brookhampton Lane, Kineton, Warwick CV35 0JB, England. A mine of practical, up-to-date information published four times during the academic year.

Appendix 4

Useful addresses

The British Council, 10 Spring Gardens, London SW1A 2BN, England.

ARELS-FELCO
(*The Association of Recognized English Language Schools – The Federation of English Language Course Organizations*), 2 Pontypool Place off Valentine Place SE1 8QF. Also organizes examinations at several levels.

BBC English by Radio and TV, Bush House, PO Box 76, London WC2B 4PH, England.